21st
Century
Skills Library

REAL WORLD MATH: GEOGRAPHY

MOUNTAINS

BY KATIE MARSICO

Published in the United States of America by
Cherry Lake Publishing, Ann Arbor, Michigan
www.cherrylakepublishing.com

Content Adviser
Andrew Dombard, Associate Professor, Department of Earth and Environmental
Sciences, University of Illinois at Chicago
Math Adviser: Tonya Walker, MA, Boston University

Credits
Photos: Cover and page 1, ©Tjerrie Smit, used under license from Shutterstock, Inc.;
page 4, ©MaxkateUSA, used under license from Shutterstock, Inc.; page 6, ©Pal
Teravagimov, used under license from Shutterstock, Inc.; page 9, ©Matyas Arvai,
used under license from Shutterstock, Inc.; page 10, ©kristian sekulic, used under
license from Shutterstock, Inc.; page 12, ©Eugene Berman, used under license
from Shutterstock, Inc.; page 15, ©Nicolas Raymond, used under license from
Shutterstock, Inc.; page 16, ©Phil Degginger/Alamy; page 19, ©Photo Resource
Hawaii/Alamy; page 20, ©enote, used under license from Shutterstock, Inc.;
page 22, ©my-summit, used under license from Shutterstock, Inc.; page 24, ©John
Warburton-Lee Photography/Alamy; page 26, ©INTERFOTO Pressebildagentur/Alamy;
page 28, ©Kapu, used under license from Shutterstock, Inc.

Library of Congress Cataloging-in-Publication Data
Marsico, Katie, 1980–
  Mountains / by Katie Marsico.
      p. cm.—(Real world math: geography)
  Includes index.
  ISBN-13: 978-1-60279-492-4
  ISBN-10: 1-60279-492-8
  1. Mountains—Juvenile literature. 2. Statistics—Juvenile literature. I. Title.
II. Series.
  GB512.M386 2010
  551.43'2—dc22   2008051508

Cherry Lake Publishing would like to acknowledge
the work of The Partnership for 21st Century Skills.
Please visit *www.21stcenturyskills.org* for more information.

TABLE OF CONTENTS

CHAPTER ONE
WHAT IS A MOUNTAIN? 4

CHAPTER TWO
**AMAZING PIECES OF
    PLANET EARTH** 10

CHAPTER THREE
**DO THE MATH: THE MIGHTY
    MAUNA LOA** 16

CHAPTER FOUR
**DO THE MATH: THE CLIMATE
    ON KILIMANJARO** 20

CHAPTER FIVE
MAKING MOUNTAINS LAST 24

REAL WORLD MATH CHALLENGE
    ANSWERS 29
GLOSSARY 30
FOR MORE INFORMATION 31
INDEX .32
ABOUT THE AUTHOR 32

CHAPTER ONE
WHAT IS A MOUNTAIN?

Do you want to feel like you are standing on top of the world? Try climbing a mountain! You may have seen mountains before. Maybe you have even skied down one. But what exactly is a mountain?

Mount Rainer is the highest peak in the Cascades.

A mountain is a landmass that rises higher than any other land around it. Most mountains have a higher **elevation** than hills. They are also usually narrower at the top, or peak, than they are at the bottom, or base.

How do mountains form? There are different ways this happens. One involves huge pieces of Earth's surface called plates. These plates can slide over or under each other. They move very slowly. The plates may slide only a few centimeters each year. That is less than the length of some paper clips! Yet the movement is enough to cause layers of rock to push up or sink down. The layers are then sometimes left towering over the surface of Earth.

A process called **erosion** can shape mountains out of the layers of rock. Erosion is when wind, water, or ice wear away land or soil. It usually takes many years for erosion to carve mountains out of the rock that is pushed up. The Alps in Europe are an example of mountains created by plate movement and erosion.

Volcanoes can also form mountains. They push out a hot liquid rock called lava when they **erupt**. The lava can build up and cause mountains to take shape. This happens over a long period of time. The Cascades in California are an example of mountains created by volcanoes.

Plate movement, erosion, and volcanoes can each play a part in forming a mountain. Even though mountains can be made in different ways, some things about them are always the same. One of these things is the way a mountain's elevation is measured. Scientists figure out the elevation by looking at the height of the **summit**, or peak. They measure how far it is above the level of the ocean's surface, called **sea level**.

Mount Everest is one of Earth's most famous landmarks.

What is the world's highest mountain peak? It's Mount Everest in the Himalayas of southern Asia. This peak rises just over 29,035 feet (8,850 meters) above sea level!

LIFE & CAREER SKILLS

Thousands of people have made it their goal to climb Mount Everest. Hundreds have succeeded. Many have died trying. The height of the peak and the freezing temperatures are just a few of the challenges. Slides of snow, ice, and mud called avalanches are another.

Stacy Allison was the first American woman to reach the peak of Mount Everest. She completed her climb in September 1988. Allison described the experience as coming to "the end of the ridge and the end of the world . . . then nothing but that clear, empty air. There was nowhere else to climb. I was standing on the top of the world."

Mountains that are connected to one another make up groups called mountain ranges. These ranges have certain land patterns in common. They all feature peaks. Most ranges also include ridges and valleys. Ridges are long, narrow strips of raised land. Valleys are lower areas of land between ridges and peaks. Rivers sometimes run through mountain valleys.

REAL WORLD MATH CHALLENGE

Is it possible for a mountain to form under water? Absolutely! Undersea mountains are called seamounts. Scientists believe there are about 100,000 seamounts in the world's oceans that measure higher than 3,281 feet. They guess there are about 30,000 seamounts in the Pacific Ocean. They also think there are about 1,000 in the Atlantic Ocean. **What percent of seamounts in the Pacific Ocean does the number of seamounts in the Atlantic Ocean represent?** Imagine a seamount that rises exactly 3,281 feet. **How much taller is Mount Everest?** (Hint: Remember that the peak of Mount Everest rises 29,035 feet).

(Turn to page 29 for the answers)

Ranges that sit close to one another often form a mountain system. Systems alongside each other are called mountain chains. Finally, groups of ranges, systems, and chains are known as belts or cordilleras.

The Pyrenees Mountains are filled with deep, beautiful valleys.

CHAPTER TWO
AMAZING PIECES OF PLANET EARTH

D id you know that mountains exist on every continent in the world? Mountains cover about 25 percent of Earth's land surface. Asia has more mountains than any other continent.

Some mountains are great places for experiencing the thrill of downhill skiing.

More than 12 percent of the people on Earth live in the mountains. What is life like for them? Mountain **climates** usually feature colder winters and cooler summers. Different sections of a mountain can have different climates. Strong winds and lower temperatures are more common in the higher parts of the mountain.

REAL WORLD MATH CHALLENGE

The highest mountain peak in Antarctica is Mount Vinson Massif, which measures 16,067 feet. The highest peak in Africa is Mount Kilimanjaro. This mountain stretches 19,340 feet tall. **How much higher is Mount Kilimanjaro than Mount Vinson Massif?** Add the elevations of the two mountains together. **How does the sum compare to the height of the tallest peak in North America?** (Hint: Mount McKinley, also known as Denali, is the tallest mountain peak in North America. It measures 20,322 feet.)

(Turn to page 29 for the answers)

How are mountains important to people who don't live in them? They may visit a mountain to take in the beautiful views or go hiking or skiing. Many tourists head to the mountains for their vacations.

Human beings also need these landmasses to survive. They use water from mountains, rivers, and lakes. About 50 percent of the people in the world rely on mountains for fresh water.

Different kinds of plants grow at different elevations on a mountain.

Many mountain ranges have rich forests, too. People need the wood from trees to do everything from make paper to build houses. The Appalachian Mountains in eastern North America are famous for forests that supply much of the country's timber.

How else are mountains important to people? Miners dig there for **minerals** such as gold, copper, iron, silver, and zinc. The Andes Mountains of South America are well known for being filled with minerals. In 2008, scientists said they believed the Andes contained 13,000 tons of gold and 250,000 tons of silver that had not even been discovered yet!

Farmers use mountains, too. Animals such as llamas, sheep, goats, and cattle feed on mountain grasses. Wild animals also live in the mountains. About 10,000 to 15,000 different kinds of plants and animals can be found in the Sierra Nevada mountains of California. These mountains are home to black bears, deer, and rattlesnakes. Primrose and sagebrush are a few examples of the many plants that grow in the Sierra Nevada.

Can you see why mountains are so important to life on Earth? You may have also noticed that measurements help people understand more about mountains. The next two chapters will show you how math plays a major part in learning about these geographic wonders!

Many llamas can be found in the Peruvian Andes near Machu Picchu.

CHAPTER THREE
DO THE MATH: THE MIGHTY MAUNA LOA

Have you ever heard of a mountain erupting? You may have if you know anything about Mauna Loa in Hawaii. *Mauna Loa* means "long mountain" in Hawaiian.

When Mauna Loa erupts, it produces a lot of fiery hot lava.

The name could not be more perfect. Mauna Loa measures 60 miles (97 km) long and 30 miles (48 km) wide and covers about 50 percent of Hawaii Island. It rises 13,680 feet (4,170 m) above sea level.

REAL WORLD MATH CHALLENGE

A mountain's summit is usually measured from where the mountain sits at sea level. Some mountains stretch much farther down and may actually touch the seafloor! Mauna Loa is such a mountain. It measures 28,680 feet from the seafloor to its summit. **How much of Mauna Loa is beneath sea level? What percentage of the mountain sits at or above sea level?** (Hint: Remember that Mauna Loa rises 13,680 feet above sea level.)

(Turn to page 29 for the answers)

People are interested in this mountain for more than its size. Mauna Loa is the world's largest active volcano. It has erupted 33 times since 1843. Scientists believe the first eruption took place between 700,000 and 1 million years ago. The last major eruption occurred in 1984.

Will another big eruption happen soon? Scientists think so. A bowl-shaped hole, or caldera, at the top of the mountain helps give clues about activity inside the volcano.

The walls of the caldera began to spread apart about 2 inches (5.1 centimeters) each year starting in 2002. This is because lava is filling the area beneath Mauna Loa's summit. Scientists believe the volcano will erupt sometime in the next few years.

LEARNING & INNOVATION SKILLS

How do we know about some of the earlier eruptions on Mauna Loa? A few brave and determined men and women took notes about what they saw when lava splashed down the mountain. The Reverend Titus Coan was one such observer. He wrote about a huge eruption on Mauna Loa in 1855. Coan and others like him were probably both amazed and scared by what they saw. His words remain important more than 100 years later as scientists try to piece together information about what Mauna Loa was like a long time ago.

The terrain of Mauna Loa makes it a great place for hiking.

REAL WORLD MATH CHALLENGE

The walls of Mauna Loa's caldera have not spread at a steady rate. Sometimes the spreading stops for weeks at a time. What if the rate were steady though? **How many inches would the walls of the caldera have spread between 2002 and 2009?** (Hint: Remember that the caldera began to spread apart at about 2 inches each year starting in 2002.)

(Turn to page 29 for the answer)

CHAPTER FOUR
DO THE MATH: THE CLIMATE ON KILIMANJARO

Have you ever visited a place that has a hot, tropical rain forest and freezing snow all in the same area? You could if you climbed Mount Kilimanjaro in Africa. You have already learned that Kilimanjaro is Africa's tallest mountain and stretches 19,340 feet (5,895 m) toward the sky in northeastern Tanzania.

Mount Kilimanjaro's size makes it visible from great distances.

Like other mountains, Mount Kilimanjaro features different climates. Temperatures are lower near the peak because the air is thinner. This makes it harder for the air to take in heat and stay warm. There is also less **precipitation** at higher elevations.

Rainfall is more common on Kilimanjaro from March through May. This period is described as the mountain's rainy season. It is the time of year when the most snow tends to fall at Kilimanjaro's peak and the greatest amount of rain usually falls at its base.

Kilimanjaro has five different climate sections, or zones. Each zone takes up about 3,000 feet (914 m) of elevation on the mountain.

REAL WORLD MATH CHALLENGE

Are you ready to climb Kilimanjaro? You had better pack a few different kinds of clothes! Temperatures at the base are usually between 70 and 80 degrees Fahrenheit. Temperatures near the peak can drop to between 0°F and –15°F. **What is the average temperature at Kilimanjaro's base? What is the average temperature at Kilimanjaro's peak?**

(Turn to page 29 for the answers)

Thick, green rain forests with tall trees and all kinds of wildlife make up the zone closest to the base. This section receives about 20 to 70 inches (51 to 178 cm) of rainfall a year. Moving upward, the second zone on Kilimanjaro features an open forest area and low-lying plants. About 40 to 79 inches (102 to 201 cm) of rain falls on this zone each year. The third zone is also like a forest and has many colorful flowers and unique-looking trees. This zone receives an average of 21 to 51 inches (53 to 130 cm) of rain every year. The zone just above this section is similar to a desert. It gets about 10 inches (25 cm) of rain a year and can be boiling hot during the day and freezing cold at night. Finally, the zone closest to the summit is

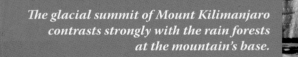

The glacial summit of Mount Kilimanjaro contrasts strongly with the rain forests at the mountain's base.

so cold that it actually has **glaciers**! This area only receives about 4 inches (10 cm) of rain and snow every year.

Each of Kilimanjaro's climate zones is home to different plants and animals. Many kinds of animals, from mice to monkeys, roam the mountain. It is hard for much to grow or live in the highest zone. The ice and cold temperatures make life there difficult.

LIFE & CAREER SKILLS

Climbing a mountain can be a dangerous adventure! It is up to you to make responsible decisions during your trip. You can only do this if you think ahead and prepare well. Check out www.climbmountkilimanjaro.com/first-time-climbers/index.html for lists of things that experts advise visitors to do before reaching Kilimanjaro. You may be surprised. Climbers often need to do everything from buying flashlights to getting shots!

A single mountain can feature a variety of environments. You will learn in the next chapter why it is important to take care of these environments. Many people are working hard to protect mountains such as Kilimanjaro.

CHAPTER FIVE
MAKING MOUNTAINS LAST

Some mountains have been around for billions of years. This does not mean that they will last or stay the same forever, though. Erosion and activity from volcanoes can change the shape of Earth's mountains. Humans cannot control these forces.

Mount Hua in China is just one of many mountain environments suffering from pollution.

REAL WORLD MATH CHALLENGE

Air pollution hurts mountain environments. You may already know that everything from cars to factories release gases that are harmful to the air. The pollution changes how clouds and the water inside them form. Less rain and snow fall. As a result, there is less water to feed the rivers and lakes in mountains. Scientists sometimes use a measurement called visibility to study air pollution in these environments. Visibility is the distance at which an object can be seen clearly. Areas with less visibility often tend to have greater air pollution. Experts believe this is the case with Mount Hua in China. Between 1954 and 2006, the amount of yearly rainfall over the mountain decreased. In 2006, scientists noted a visibility of only 12.4 miles at Mount Hua's summit. In 1954, the visibility was 23.6 miles. **What was the difference in visibility at Mount Hua's summit between 1954 and 2006?**

(Turn to page 29 for the answer)

However, it is up to humans to take care of mountains. One way we can do this is by trying to stop **pollution** and any other harm to mountain environments. People can take simple steps

such as putting out campfires and cleaning up trash when they
visit mountains. A forest fire can kill or injure wildlife. Garbage
can have the same effect and also pollutes rivers and lakes.

Many groups have formed to protect mountain environments. They try to help everyone understand that the
mountains' rivers, lakes, and forests will not last forever if
humans waste water or cut down too many trees.

*Trash, such as these glass bottles, is harmful
to the natural environment of the Himalayas.*

Even digging for minerals can be harmful to mountain environments. The miners can destroy plants and bother wildlife. Mining can also pollute rivers and lakes.

What can you do to preserve the world's mountains? Use your math skills to learn more about these towering landforms.

Be sure to clean up after yourself whenever you go for a hike or ski. Think about joining a group that protects mountain environments. There are many ways you can do your part!

As long as we take care of them, the world's mountains will continue to provide resources, habitats, and exciting places to explore.

REAL WORLD MATH CHALLENGE ANSWERS

Chapter One

Page 8
The seamounts in the Atlantic Ocean represent about 3% of seamounts in the Pacific Ocean.
1,000 ÷ 30,000 = 0.03 = 3%
Mount Everest rises 25,754 feet (7,850 m) higher than the seamount described.
29,035 feet – 3,281 feet = 25,754 feet

Chapter Two

Page 11
Mount Kilimanjaro is 3,273 feet (998 m) taller than Mount Vinson Massif.
19,340 feet – 16,067 feet = 3,273 feet
The total of the two elevations is 35,407 feet (10,792 m).
16,067 feet + 19,340 feet = 35,407 feet
The total of the two elevations is 15,085 feet (4,598 m) higher than Mount McKinley.
35,407 feet – 20,322 feet = 15,085 feet

Chapter Three

Page 17
Exactly 15,000 feet (4,572 m) of Mauna Loa is below sea level.

28,680 feet – 13,680 feet = 15,000 feet
About 48% of the mountain sits at or above sea level.
13,680 ÷ 28,680 = 0.476 = 48%

Page 19
The walls of the caldera would have spread 14 inches (36 cm) from 2002 to 2009.
7 years x 2 inches per year = 14 inches

Chapter Four

Page 21
The average temperature at Kilimanjaro's base is 75°F (24°C).
70° + 80° = 150°
150° ÷ 2 = 75°F
The average temperature at Kilimanjaro's peak is –7.5°F (–22°C).
0° + –15° = –15°
–15° ÷ 2 = –7.5°F

Chapter Five

Page 25
The difference in visibility between 1954 and 2006 was 11.2 miles (18 km).
23.6 miles – 12.4 miles = 11.2 miles

GLOSSARY

climates (KLY-metz) the average weather in different areas over a long period of time

elevation (eh-luh-VAY-shuhn) the height or distance of something above a certain point such as sea level

environment (en-VYE-ruhn-ment) an area in which people, animals, and plants live and grow

erosion (ih-ROH-zhuhn) a process in which wind, water, or ice wear away land or soil

erupt (ih-RUPT) to suddenly release lava and rock

glaciers (GLAY-shurz) large masses of ice that move very slowly

minerals (MIN-er-ulz) substances such as gold or silver that have certain chemical features

pollution (puh-LOO-shuhn) dirt, waste, or chemicals that harm the environment

precipitation (pri-sip-i-TAY-shuhn) the rain, sleet, hail, or snow that falls to the surface of Earth

sea level (SEE LEH-vuhl) the surface of the ocean

summit (SUH-mit) the peak or highest point on a mountain

FOR MORE INFORMATION

BOOKS

Chambers, Catherine, and Nicholas Lapthorn. *Mountains*. Chicago: Heinemann, 2007.

Tidmarsh, Celia. *Mountains*. San Diego: Blackbirch Press, 2004.

Watson, Galadriel Findlay. *Mount Kilimanjaro*. New York: Weigl Publishers, 2008.

Webster, Christine. *Mauna Loa: The Largest Volcano in the United States*. New York: Weigl Publishers, 2004.

WEB SITES

The Mountain Institute: Learning About Mountains
www.mountain.org/education/
Read more about mountains and the plants, animals, and people that live on them

Rocky Mountains—Science for Kids!
www.historyforkids.org/scienceforkids/geology/platetectonics/rockies.htm
Learn more about how the Rocky Mountains formed

INDEX

Africa, 11, 20–21
Alps Range, 5
Andes Mountains, 14
Antarctica, 11
Appalachian Mountains, 13
Asia, 6, 10
Atlantic Ocean, 8
avalanches, 6

bases, 5, 21, 22

caldera, 17–18, 19
Cascade Range, 5
climate, 11, 21–23, 27, 28
continents, 10, 11
cordilleras, 8

elevation, 5, 6, 11, 17, 22
erosion, 5, 24
eruptions, 5, 16, 17, 18

forests, 13, 20, 22, 26
formation, 5, 8

glaciers, 22–23, 27
global warming, 27

Himalayan Range, 6

lava, 5, 18

Mauna Loa volcano, 16–18, 19
mining, 14, 27
mountain climbing, 4, 6, 20, 21, 23
mountain ranges, 7–8, 13
mountain systems, 8
Mount Everest, 6, 8
Mount Hua, 25
Mount Kilimanjaro, 11, 20–23
Mount McKinley, 11
Mount Vinson Massif, 11

Pacific Ocean, 8
peaks, 5, 6, 7, 8, 11, 17, 18, 21, 22–23, 25
plant life, 13, 14, 22, 23, 27
plates, 5
pollution, 25–26, 27
precipitation, 21, 22, 25
preservation, 25–28

ridges, 7–8

sea level, 6, 17
seamounts, 8
Sierra Nevada Range, 13, 14

valleys, 7, 8
volcanoes, 5, 16–18, 19, 24

water, 5, 8, 12, 25, 26, 27
wildlife, 13, 14, 22, 23, 26, 27

ABOUT THE AUTHOR

Katie Marsico worked as a managing editor in children's publishing before becoming a freelance writer. She lives near Chicago, Illinois, with her husband and children. She dedicates this book to her uncle, geology expert Joe Rice.